# Animals at Home

By Donna Latham
Illustrated by John Sandford

**Target Skill** *Review*
**High-Frequency Words** *Review*

PEARSON

Scott
Foresman

It is a big nest.

Can you spot the egg in it?

What can rest in the nest? A hen!

It is a pen.

What can get fed in the pen?

A big pig and a little pig!

It is a big den.

What will stop in the den to rest?

Can you tell what it is?

See the big web in the hot sun.

What can sit in the web?

Can you tell what it is?

Here is a bat.

The bat can drop from the top.

Can you tell where the bat is?

Here is a blue fish.

It can swim and swim.

Can you tell where the fish is?

It can set up a nest in the grass.

A little one set up a hill here.

What is it? An ant!